LETTER TRACING FOR KIDS

BENTLEY

TRACE MY NAME WORKBOOK

Can't Find Your Name?

Have our elves create a personalized book
with the name of your choice today!

VISIT US AT:
PERSONALIZETHISBOOK.COM

Chiquita publishing

Cover and page design by Cool Journals Studios - Copyright 2017

ABOUT ME

MY NAME IS:

Bentley

I LIVE IN:

_____

- - - - - - - - - - - - - - - - - - - -

For parents

- - - - - - - - - - - - - - - - - - - -

_____

For kids

I AM [ ] YEARS OLD.

DRAW YOU AND YOUR FAMILY

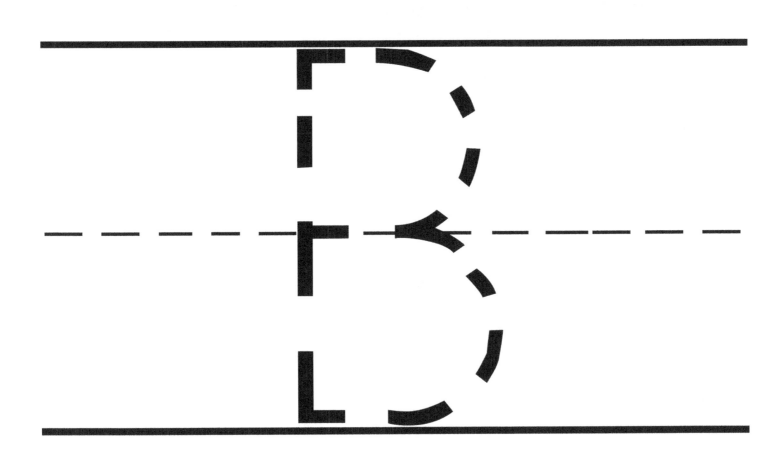

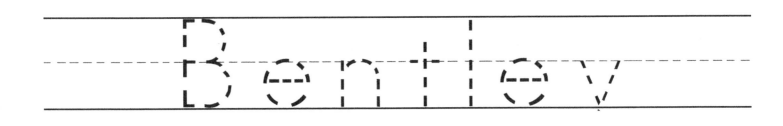

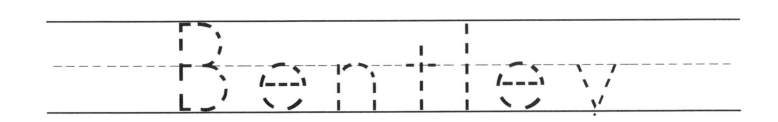

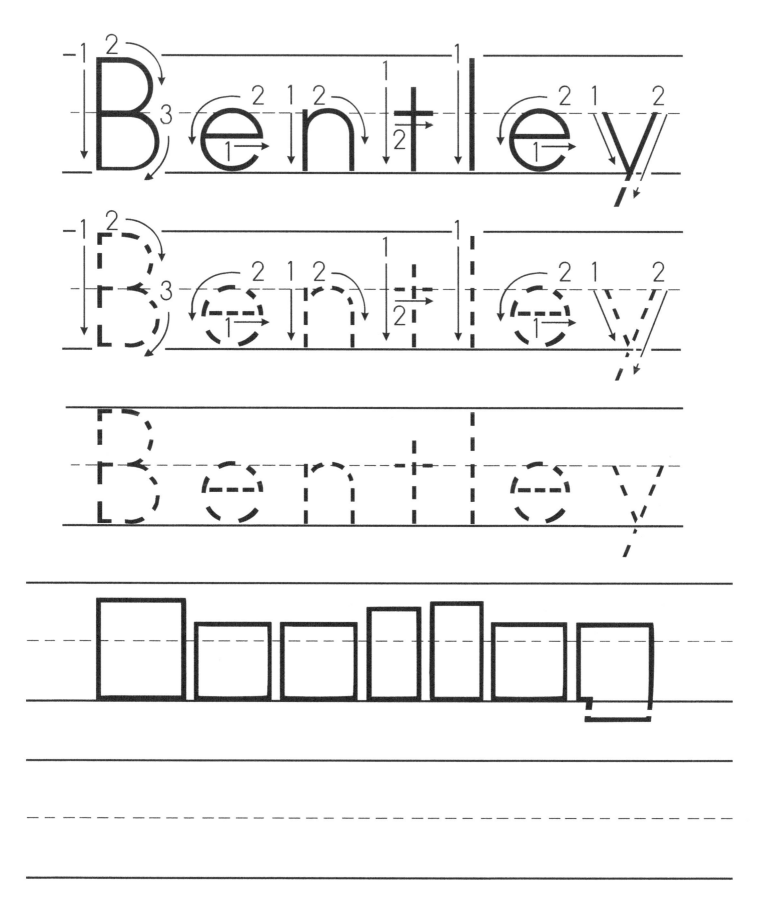

THIS IS HOW I WRITE MY NAME

MY NAME HAS ___ LETTERS

1	2	3	4	5	6	7	8

Bentley

_____ entley

_____ ntley

_____ tley

_____ ley

_____ ey

_____

COLOR THE EGGS WITH LETTERS OF OUR NAME WRITE YOUR NAME

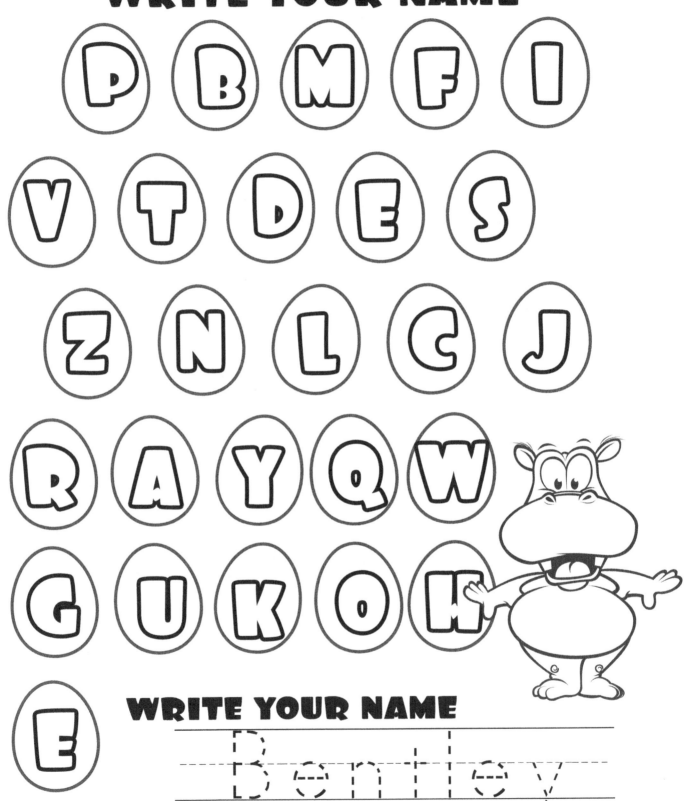

P B M F I

V T D E S

Z N L C J

R A Y Q W

G U K O H

E

WRITE YOUR NAME

Bentley

WRITE YOU NAME WITH,

PEN

Bentley

CRAYON

Bentley

WRITE YOUR NAME IN BLUE

Bentley

WRITE YOUR NAME IN YELLOW

Bentley

DRAW YOUR
FAVORITE THINGS

COLOR

FOOD

TOY

ANIMAL

MY NAME

My name starts with	My name ends with
_____	_____

FILL THE LETTERS OF YOUR NAME WHITH DIFFERENT COLORS

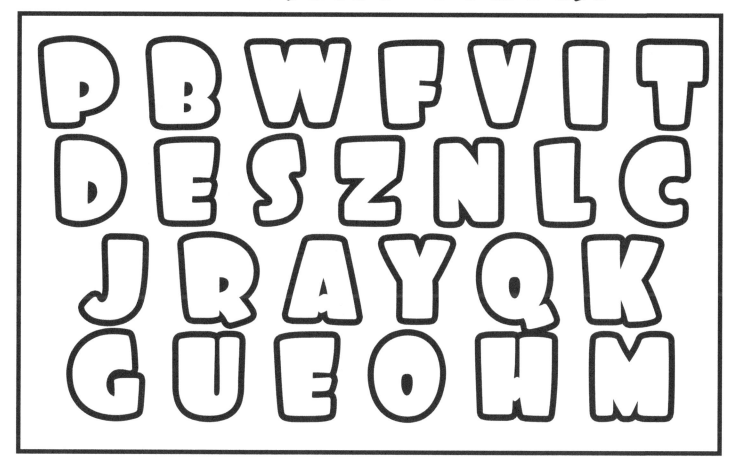

P B W F V I T
D E S Z N L C
J R A Y Q K
G U E O H M

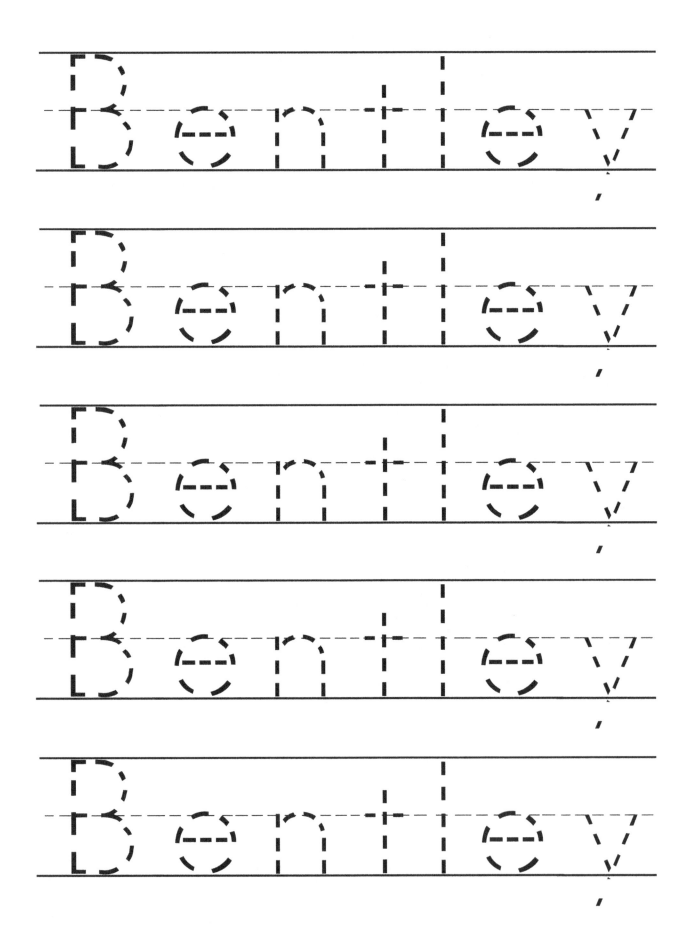

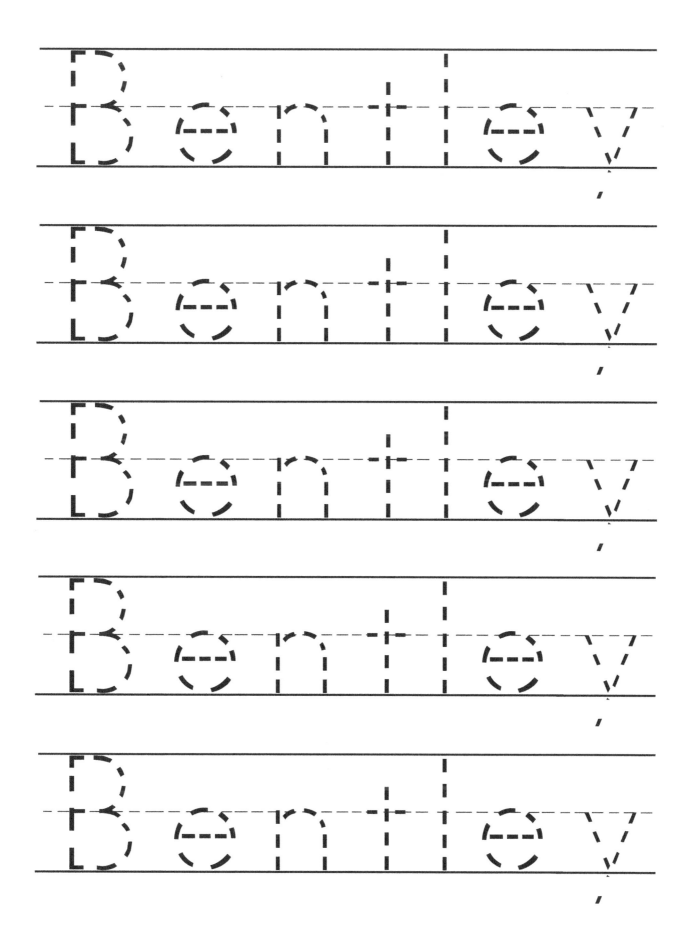

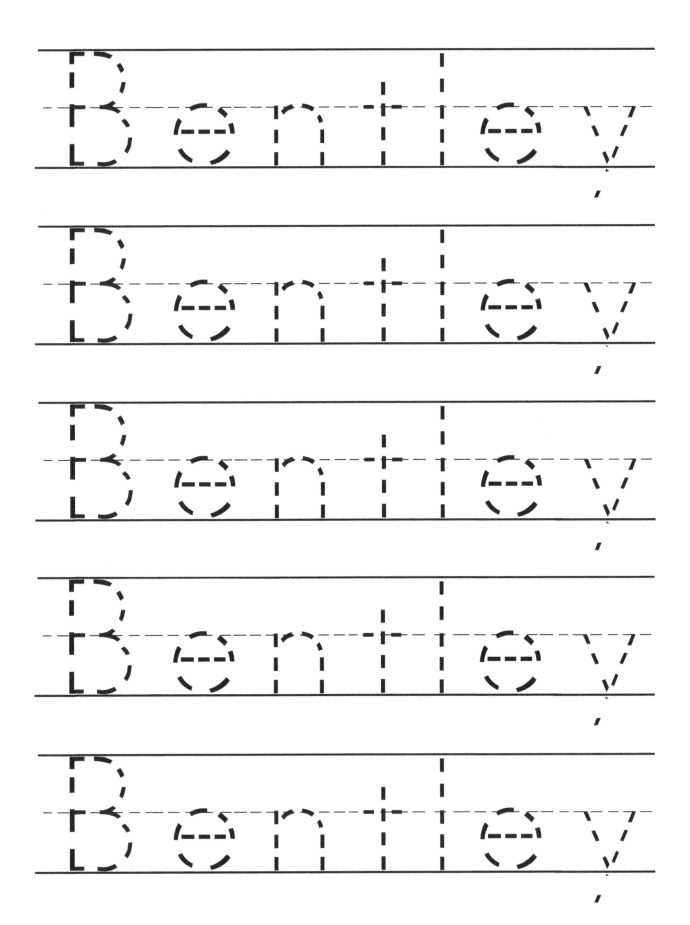

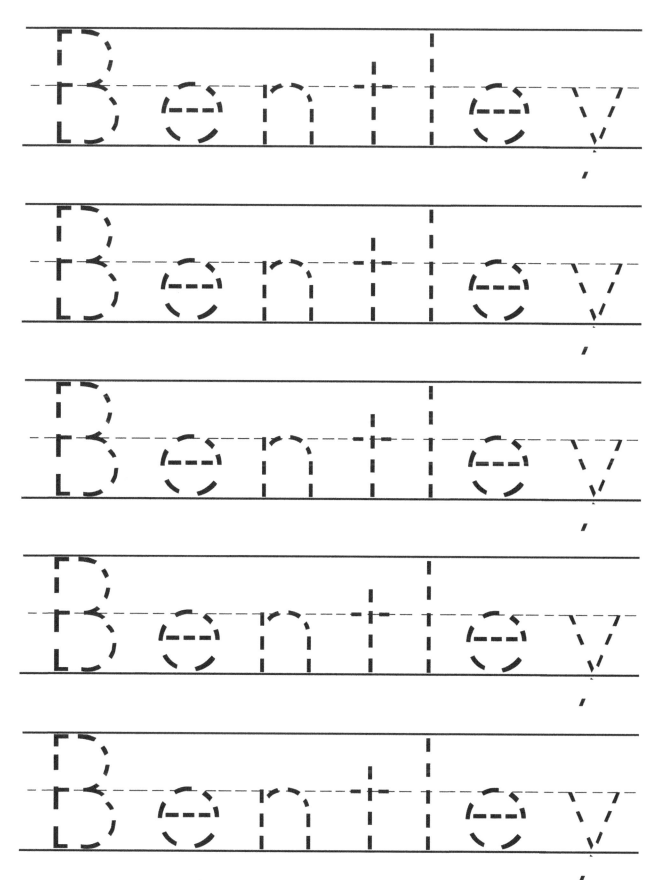

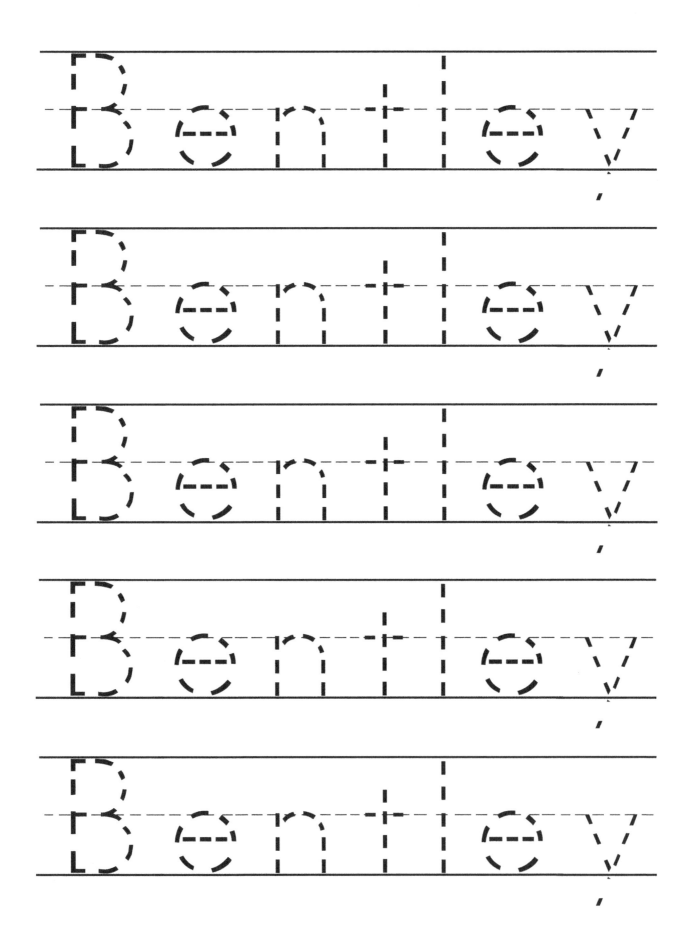

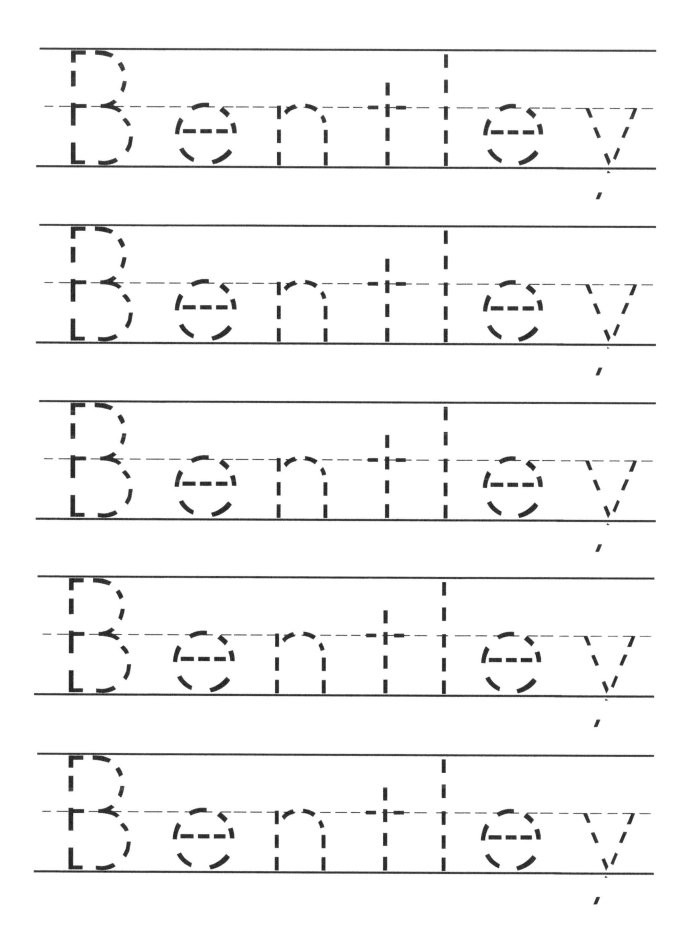

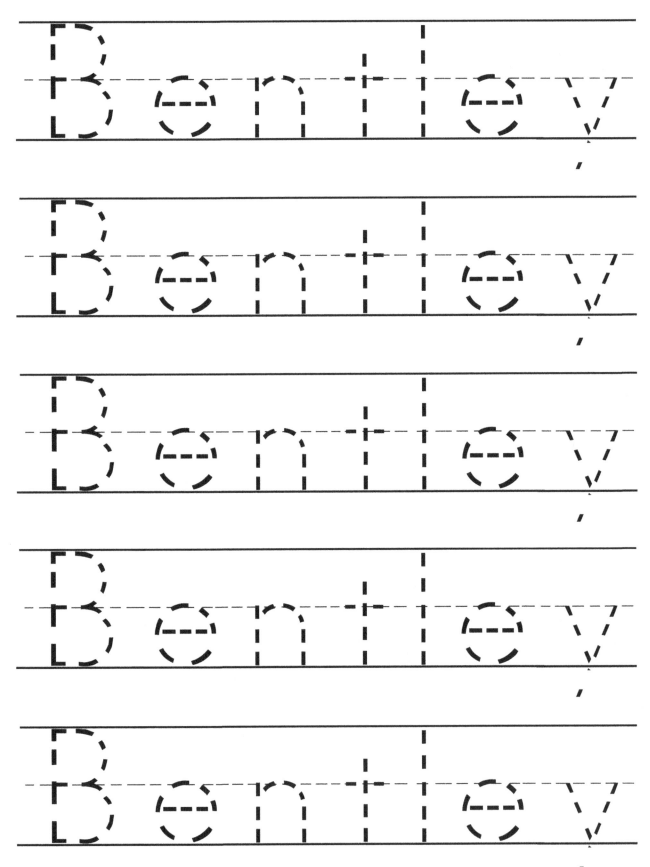

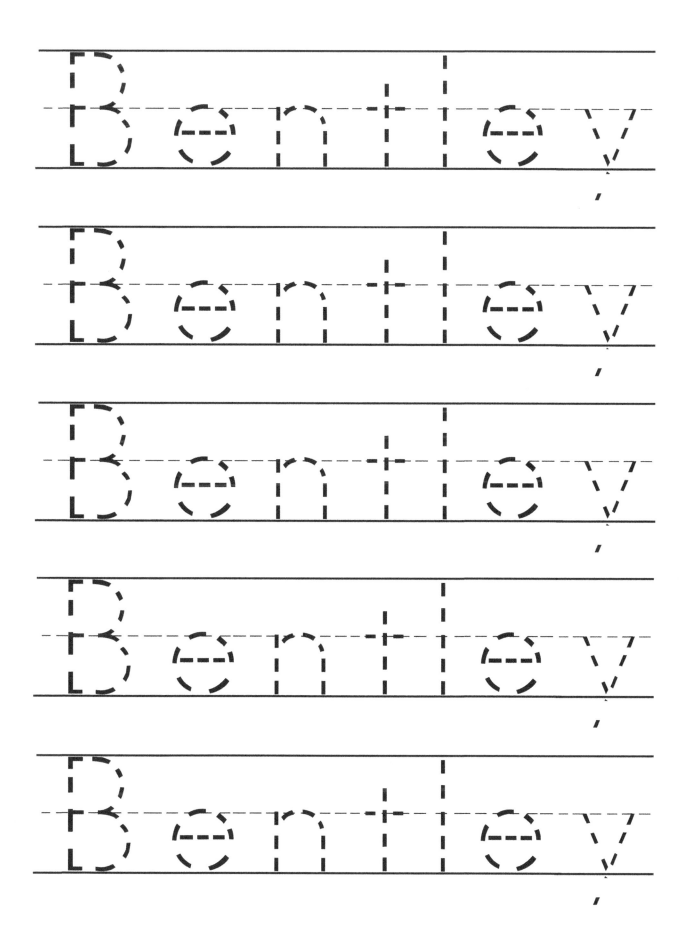

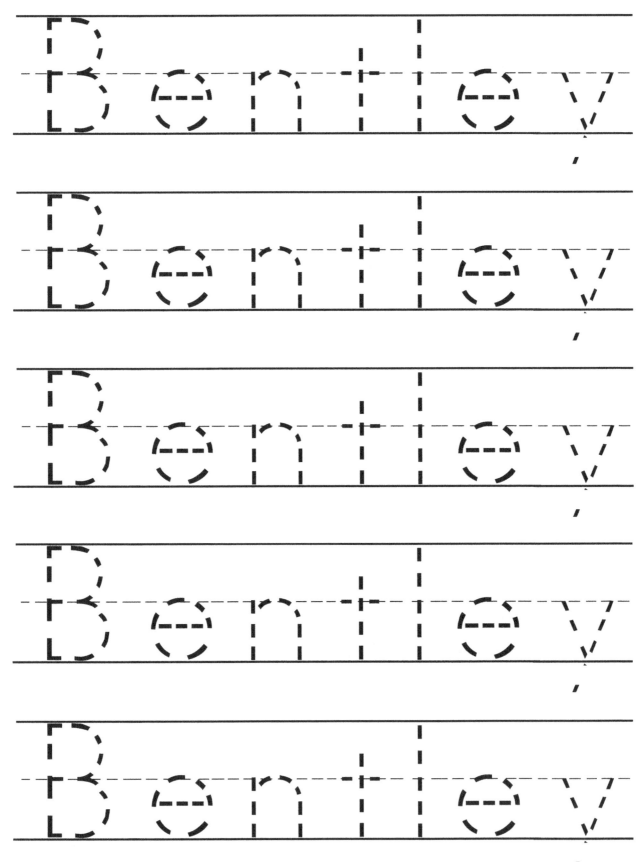

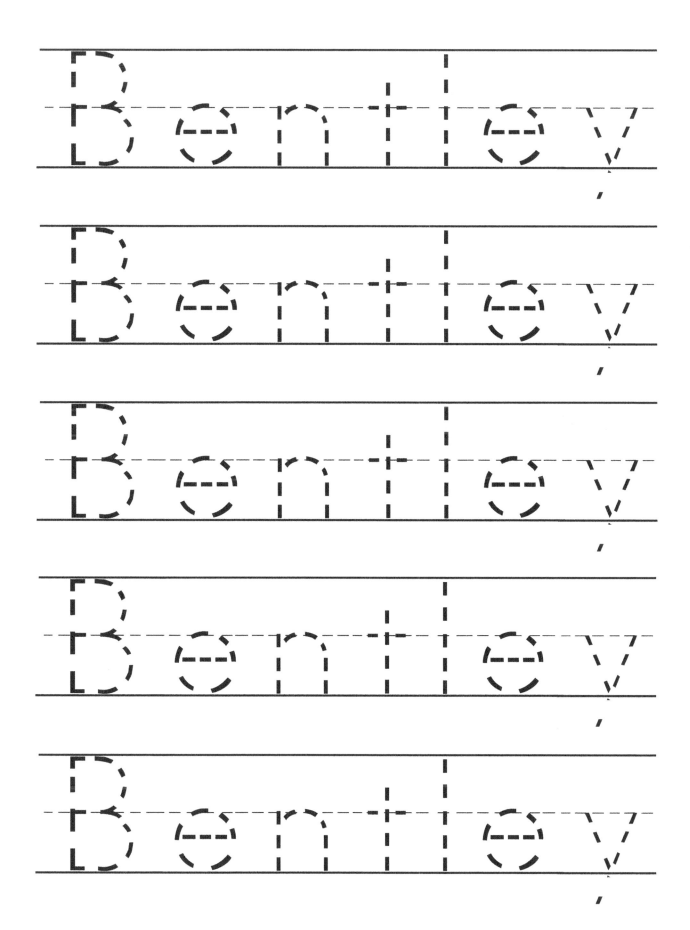

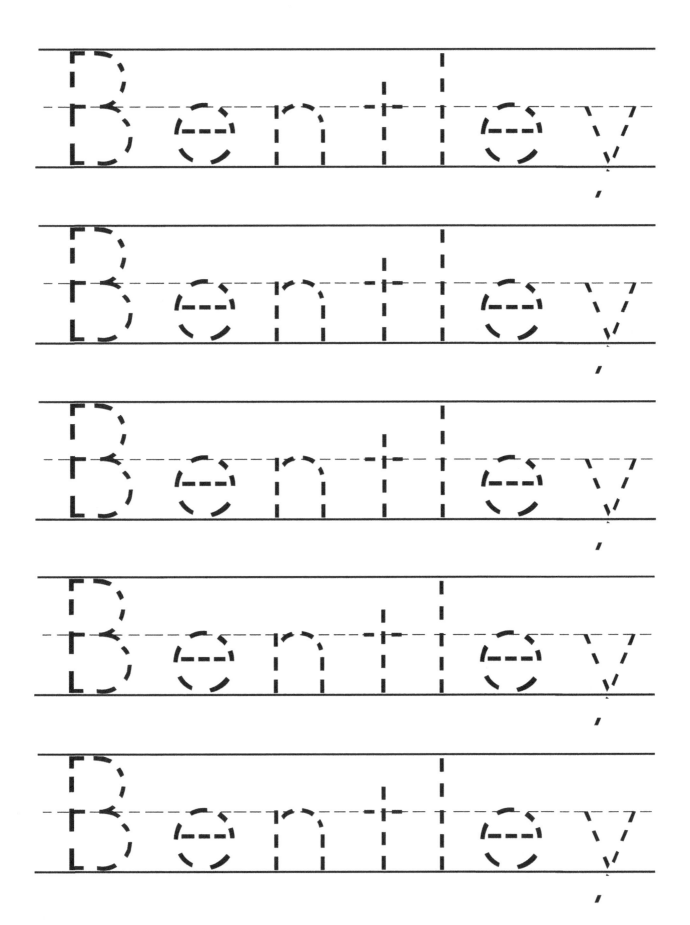

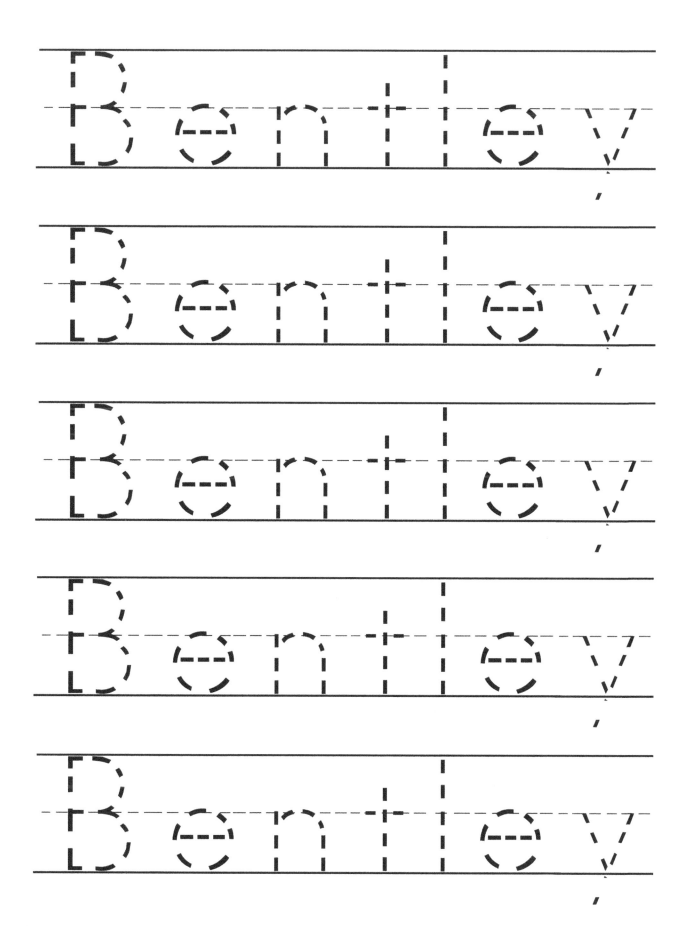

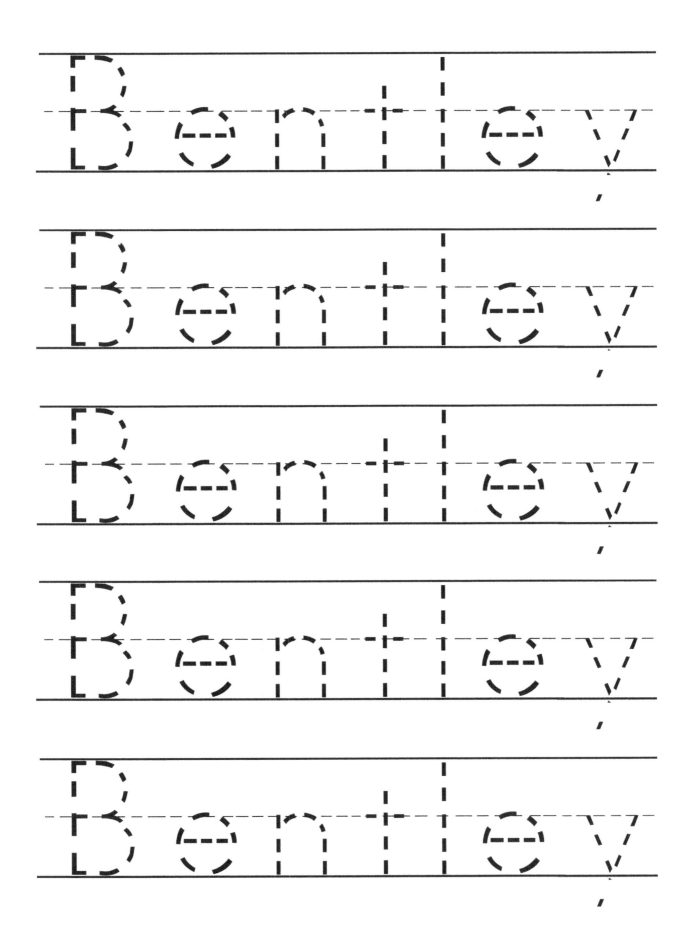

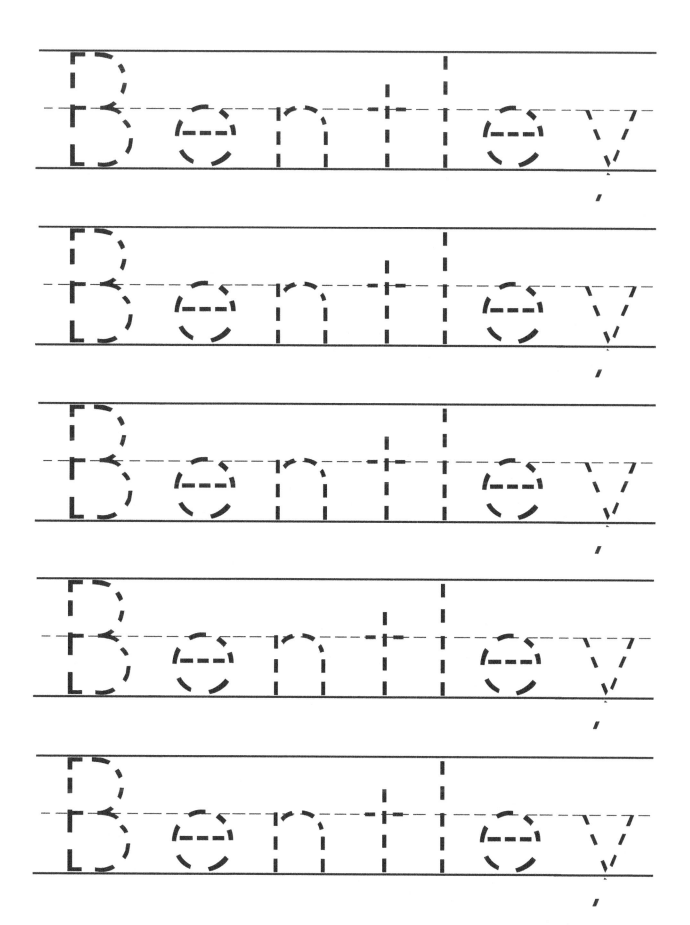

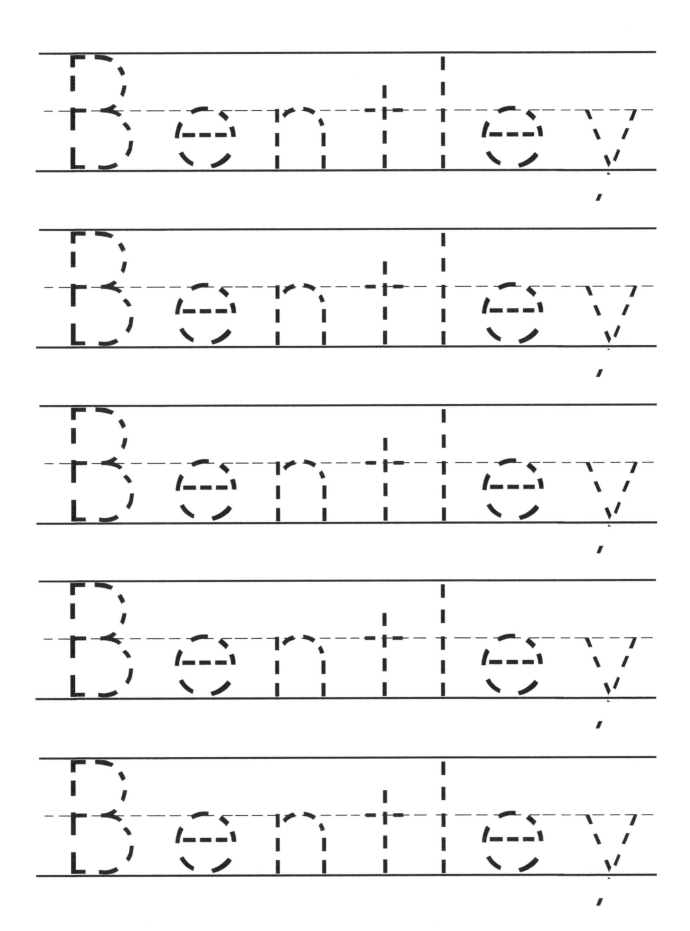

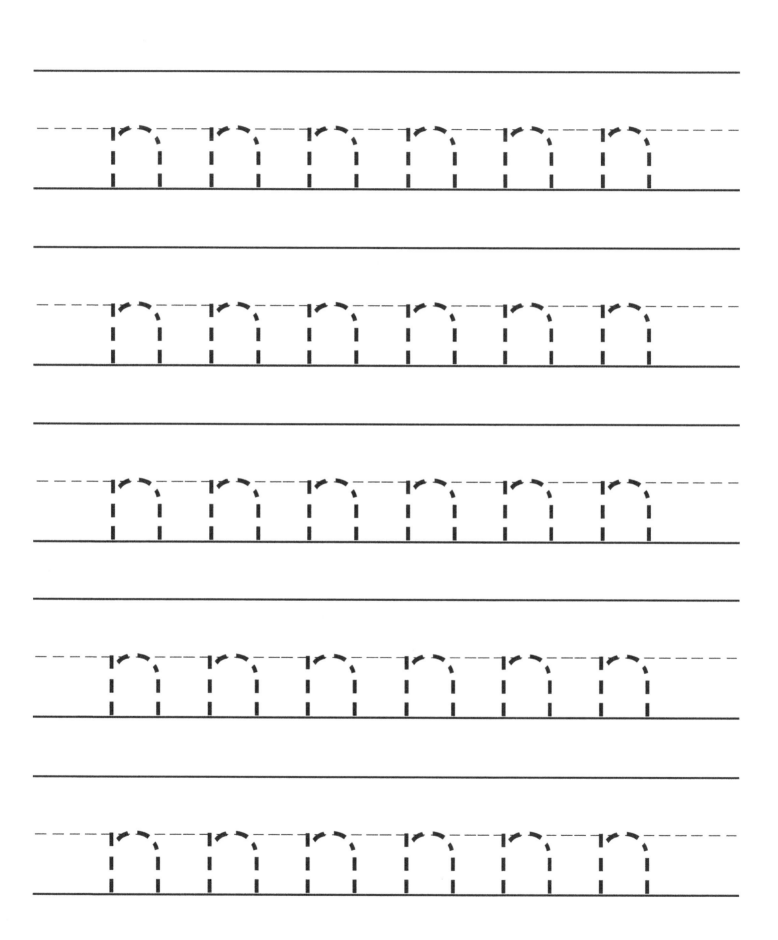

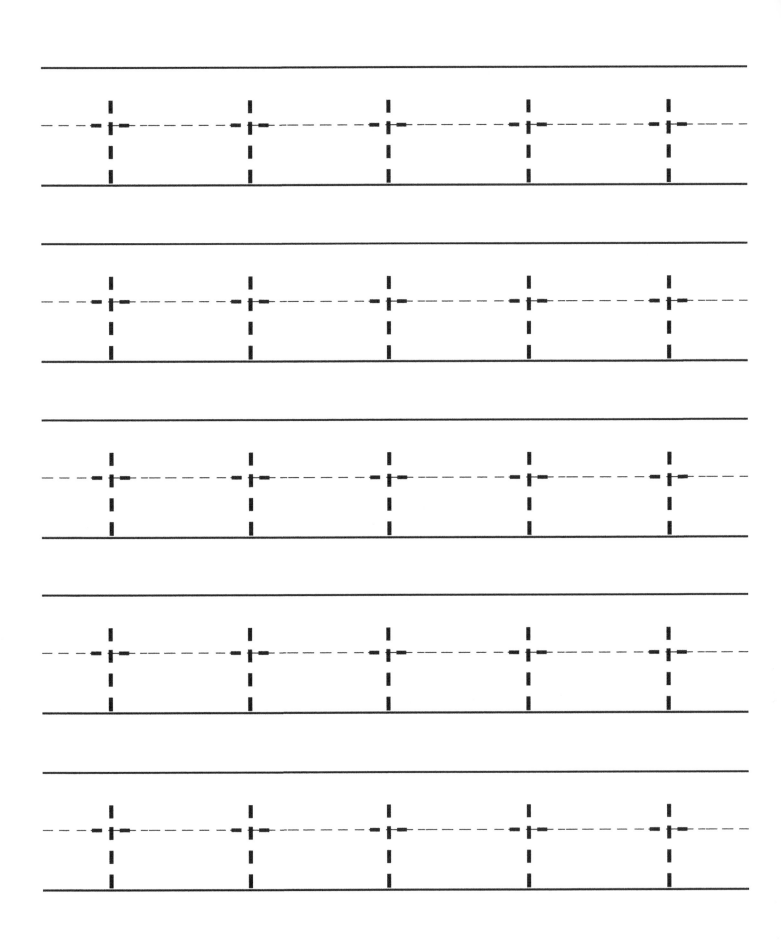

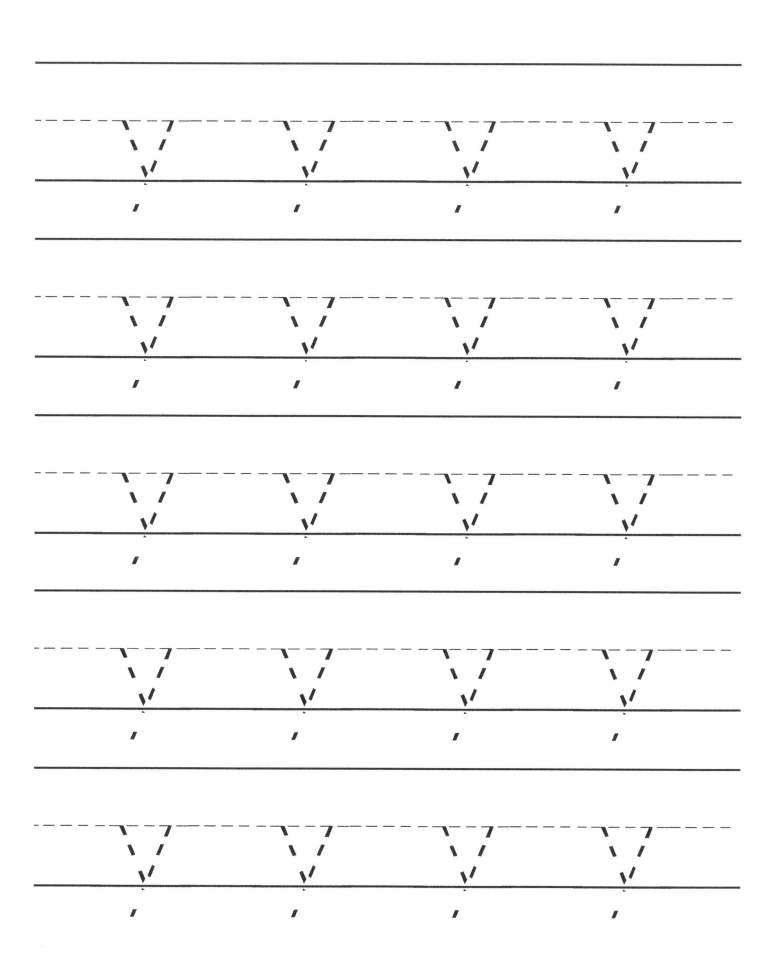

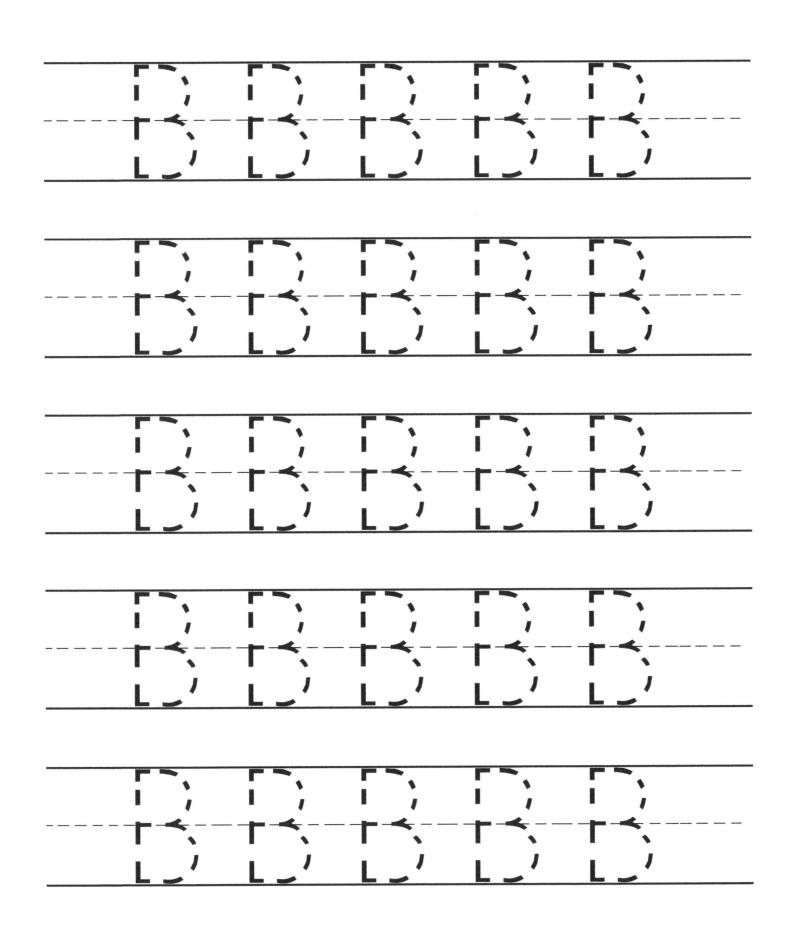

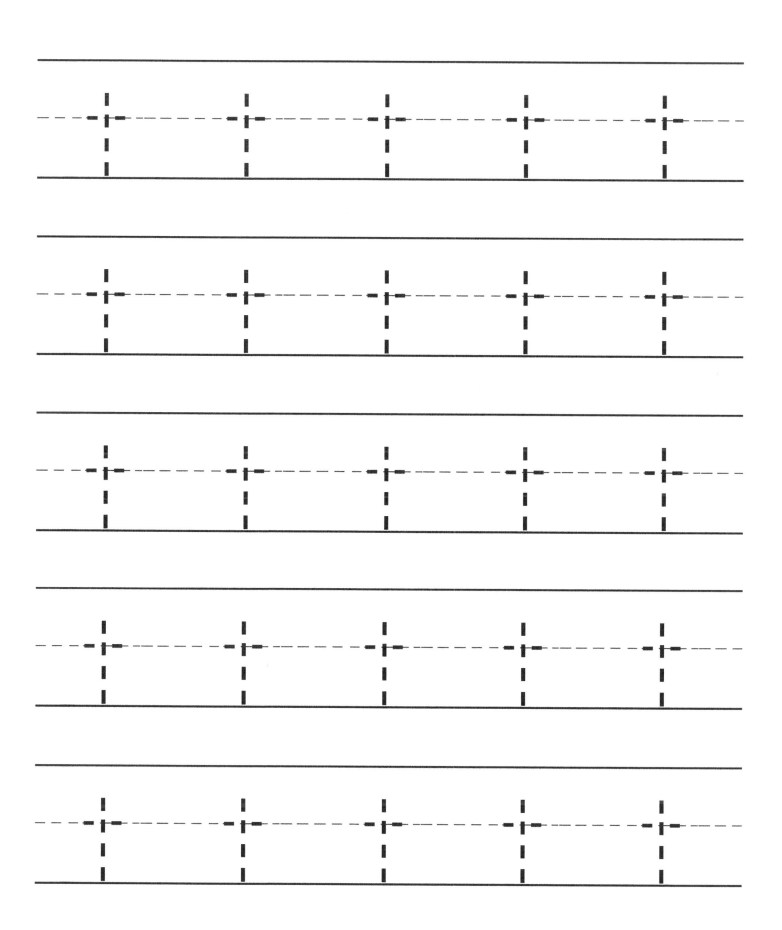

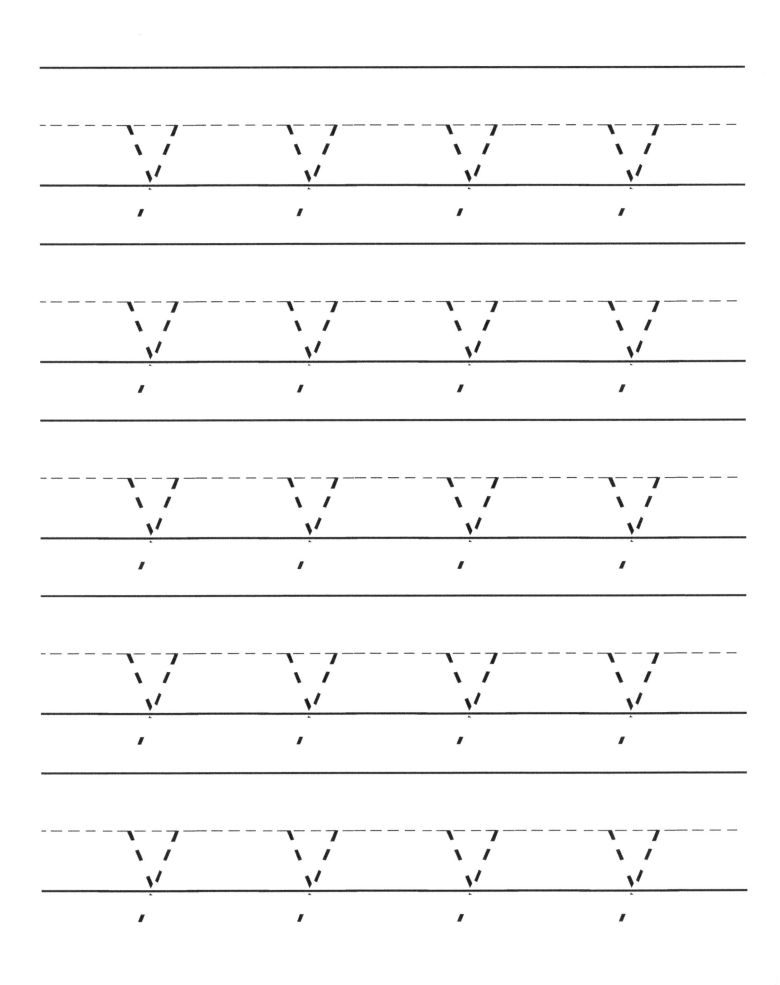

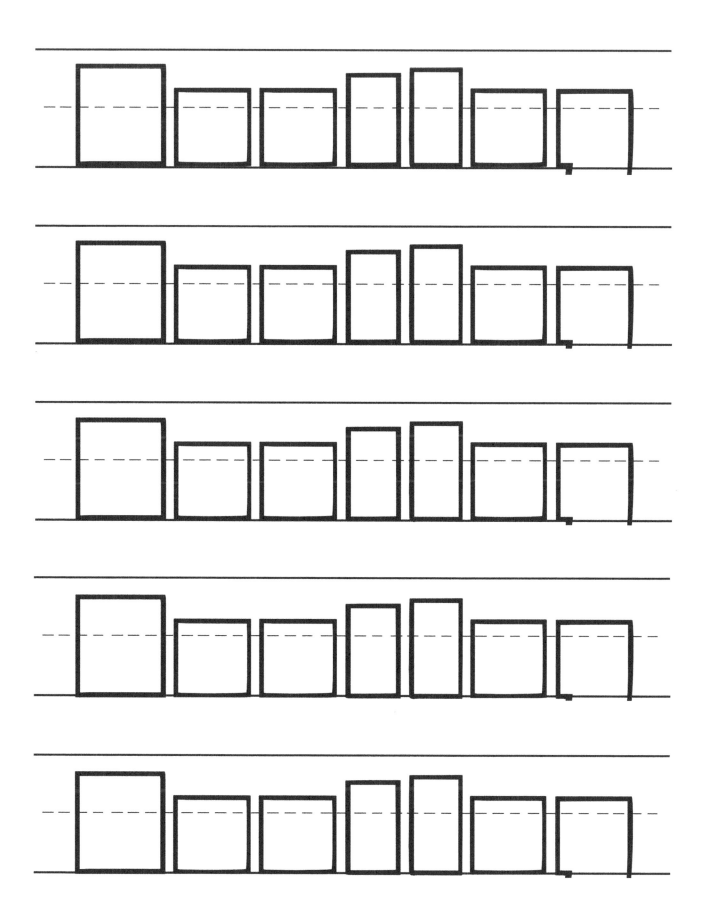

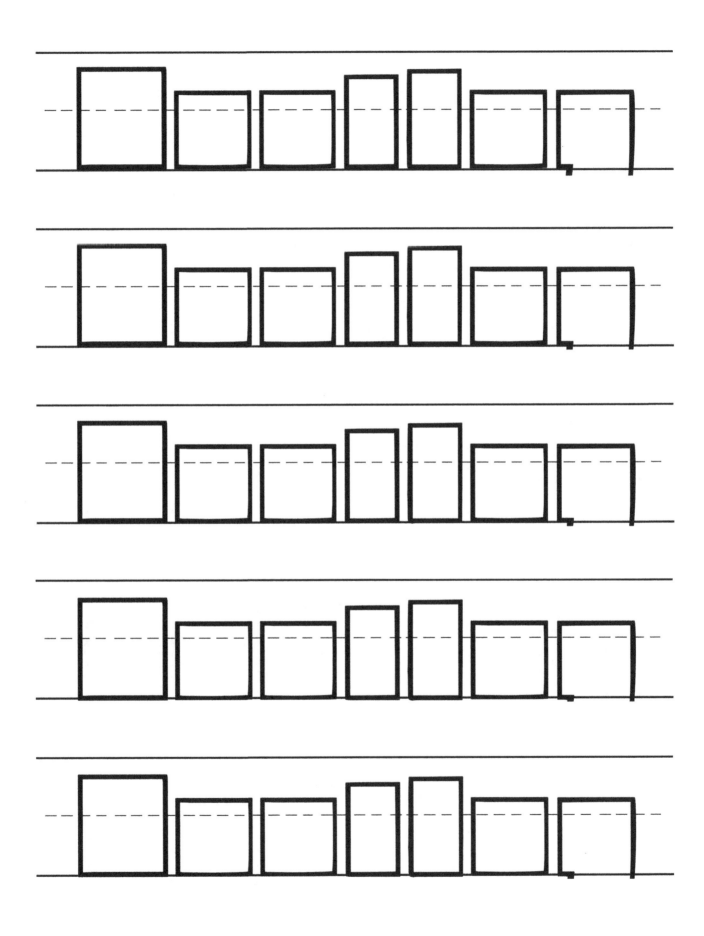

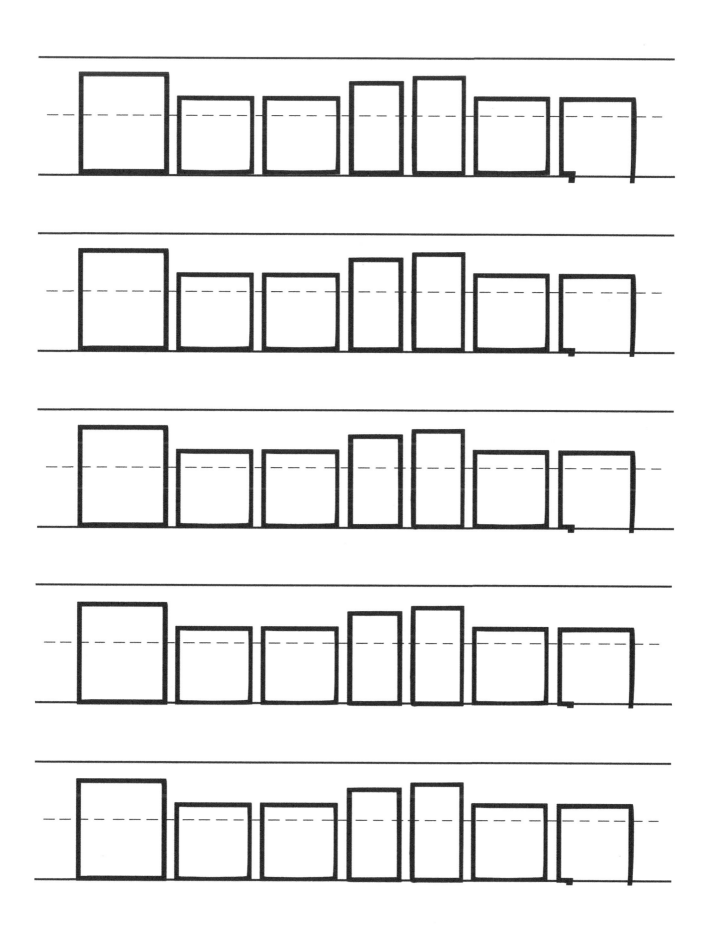

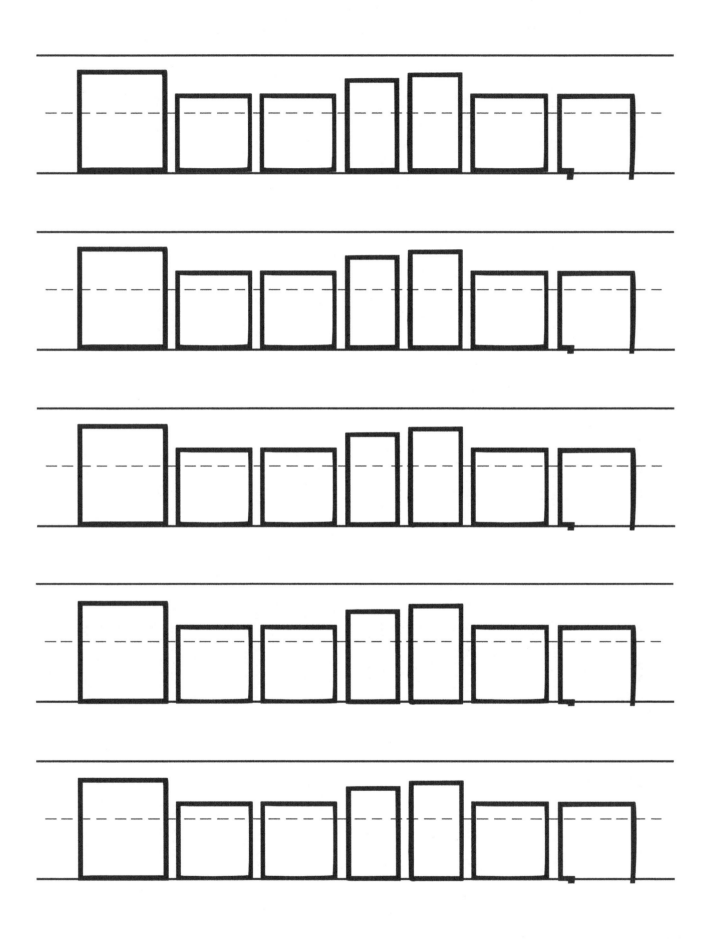

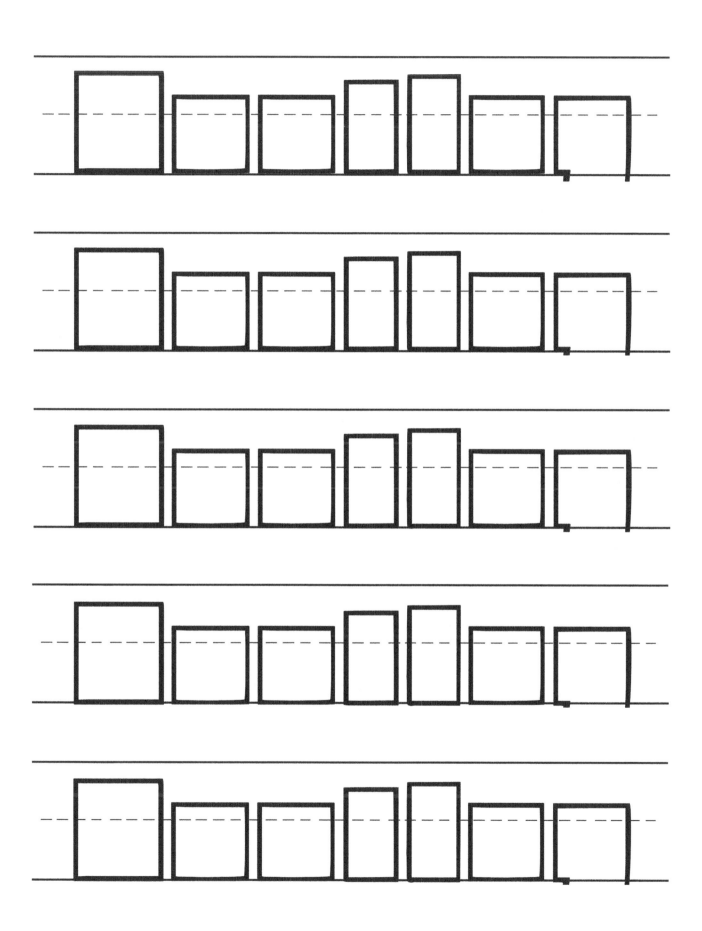

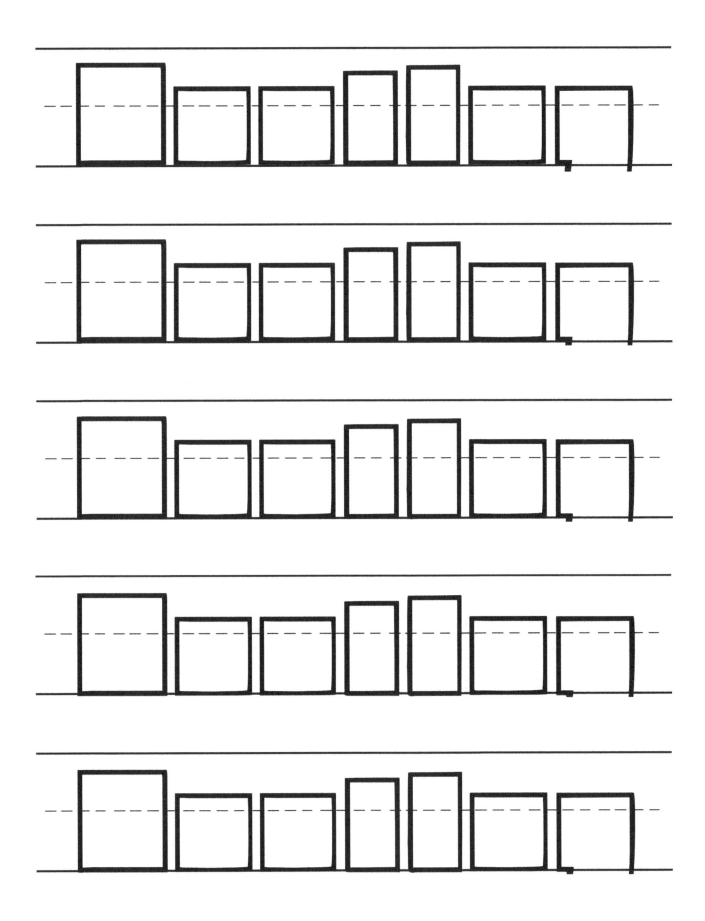

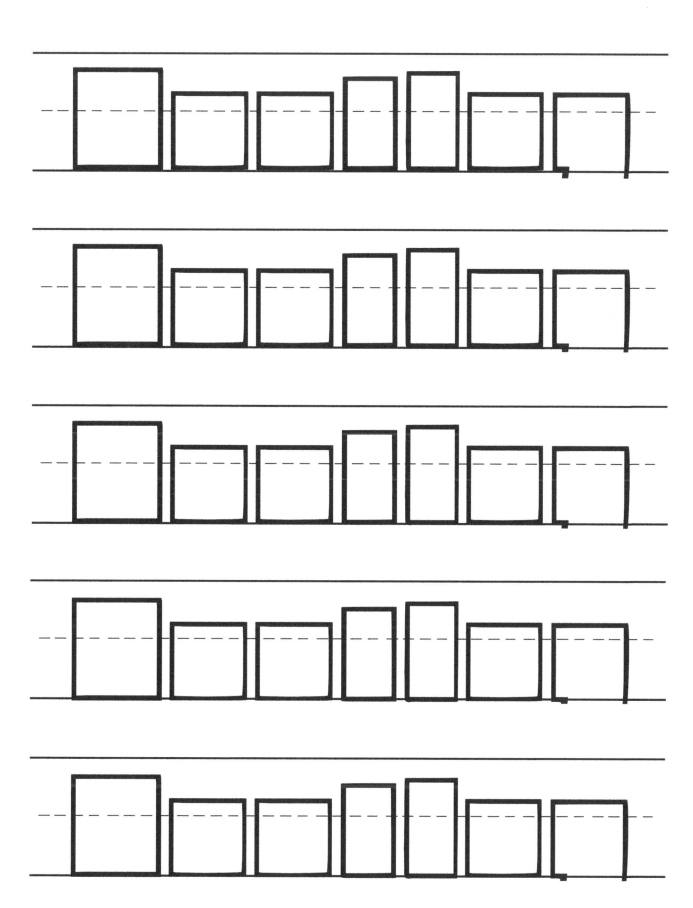

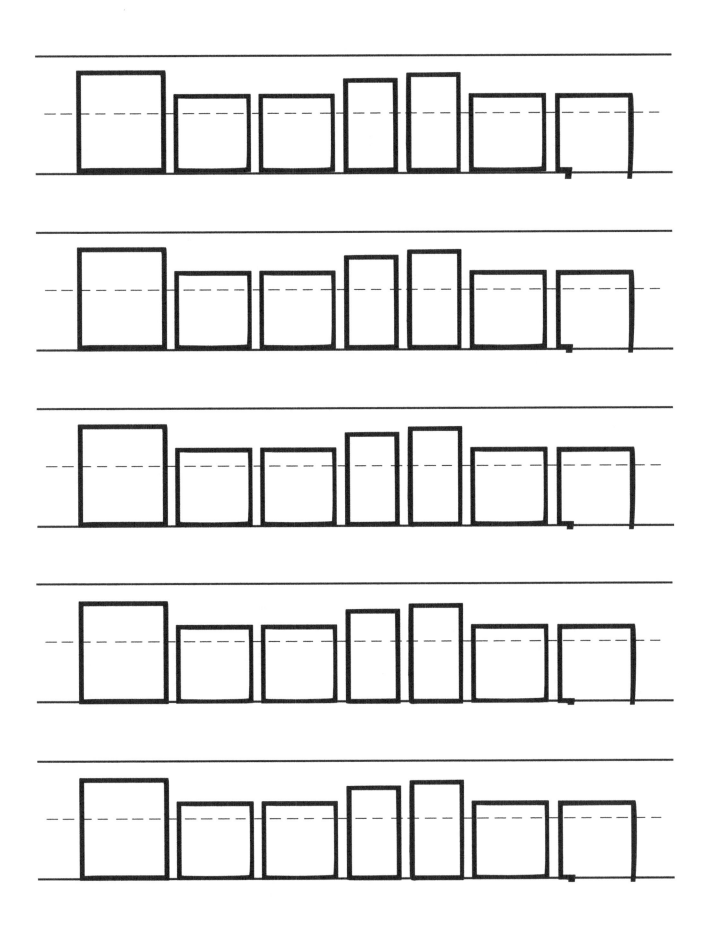

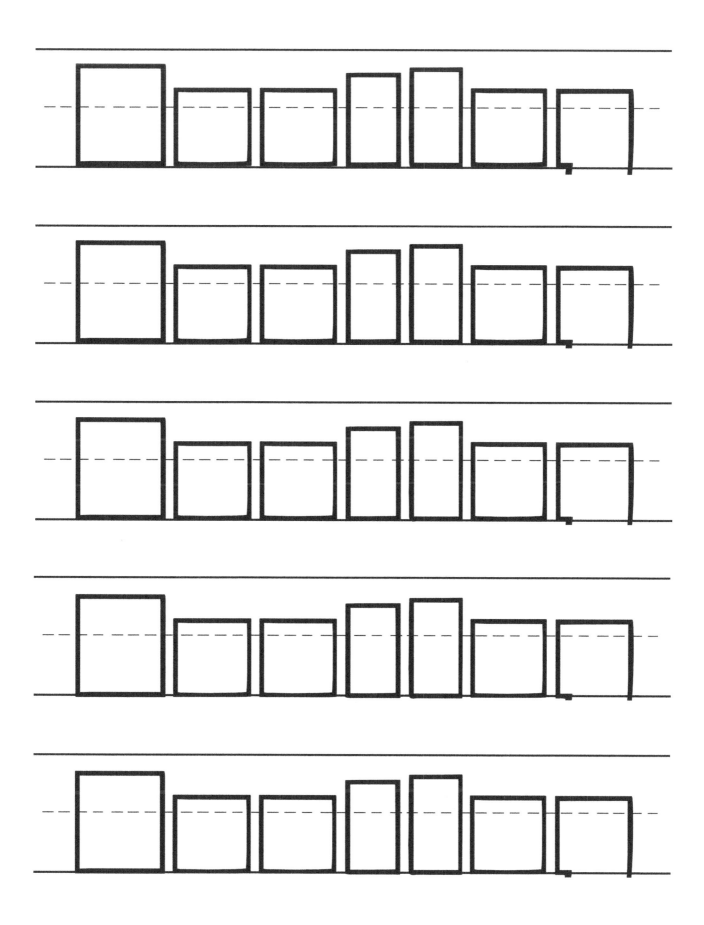

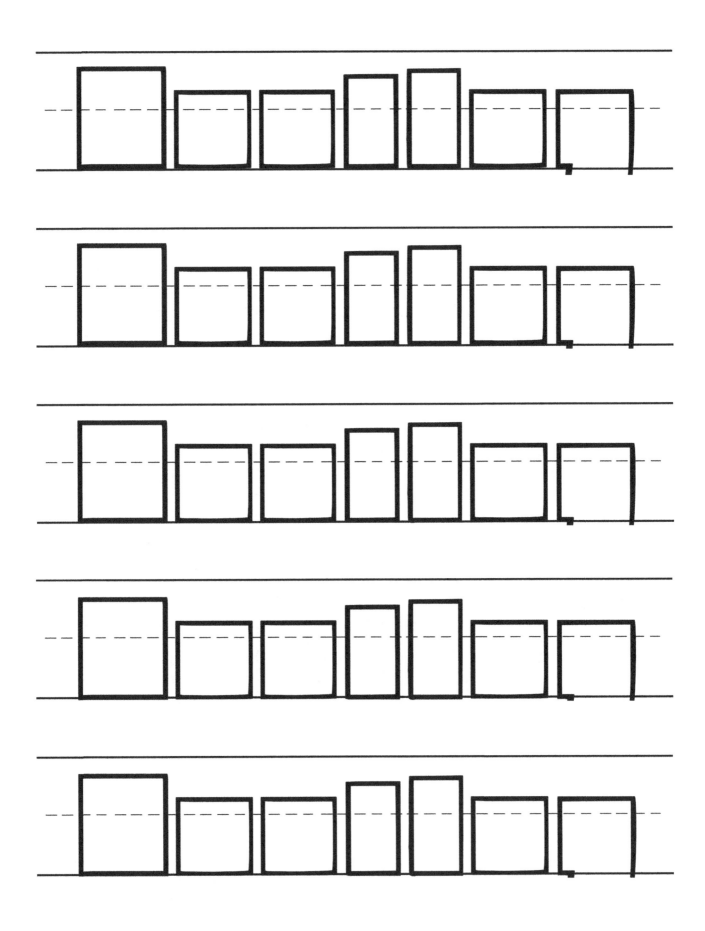

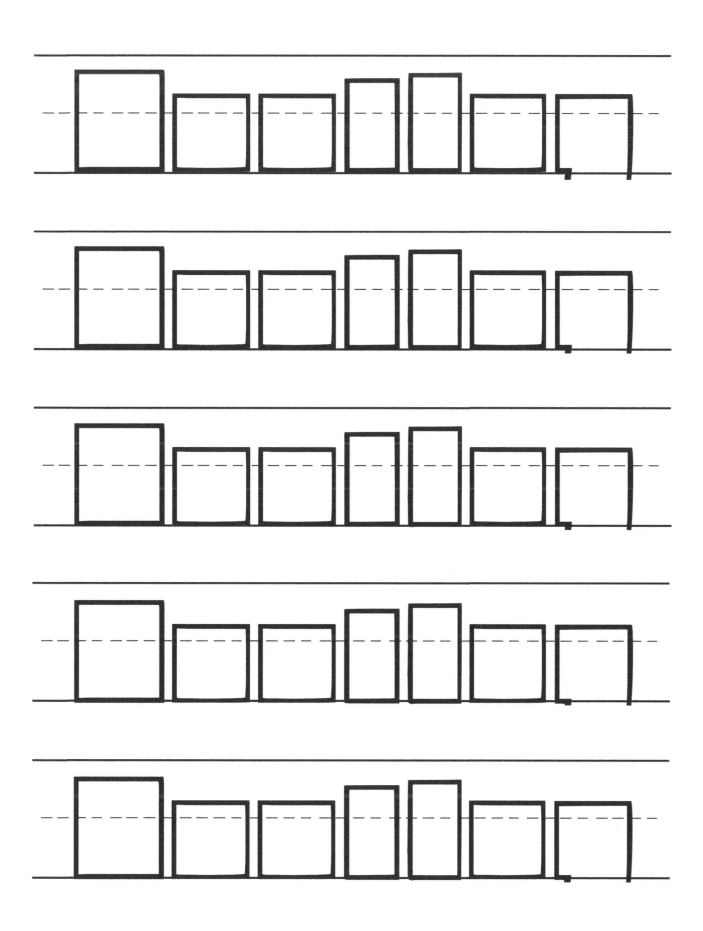

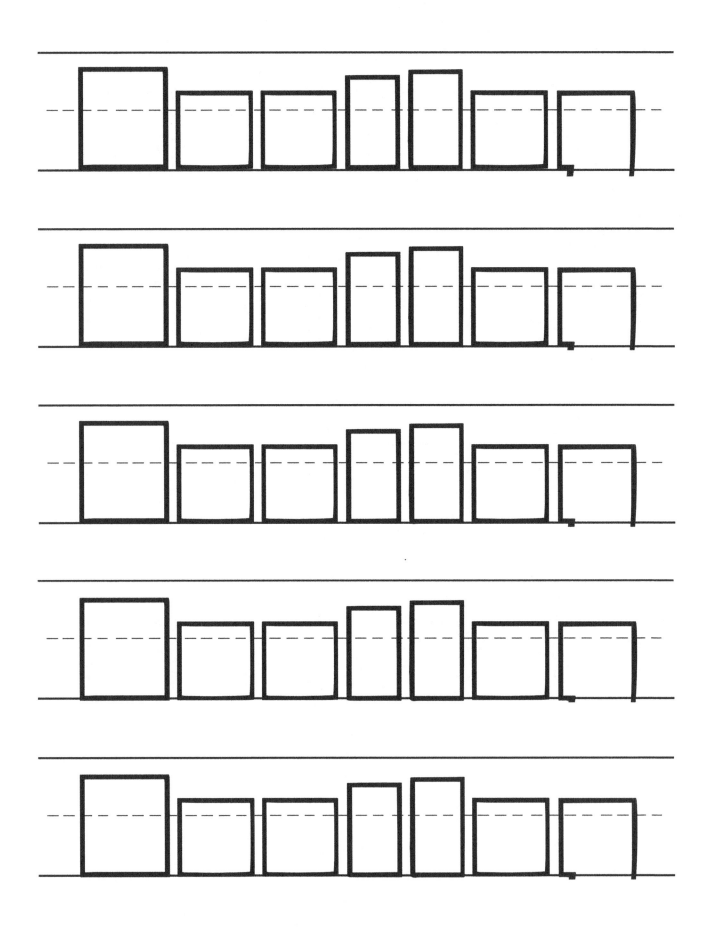

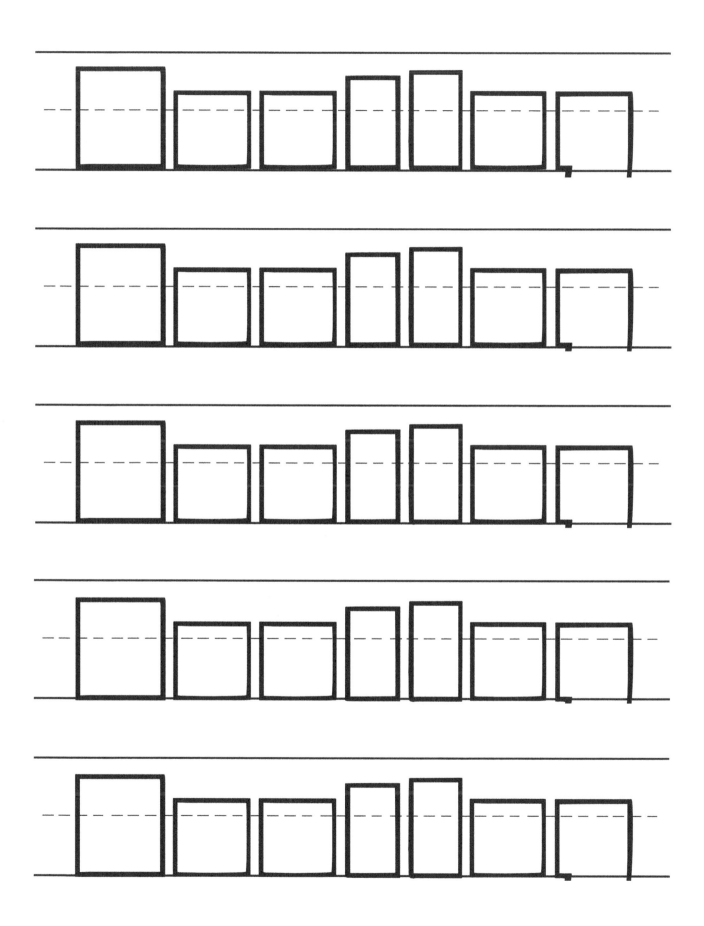

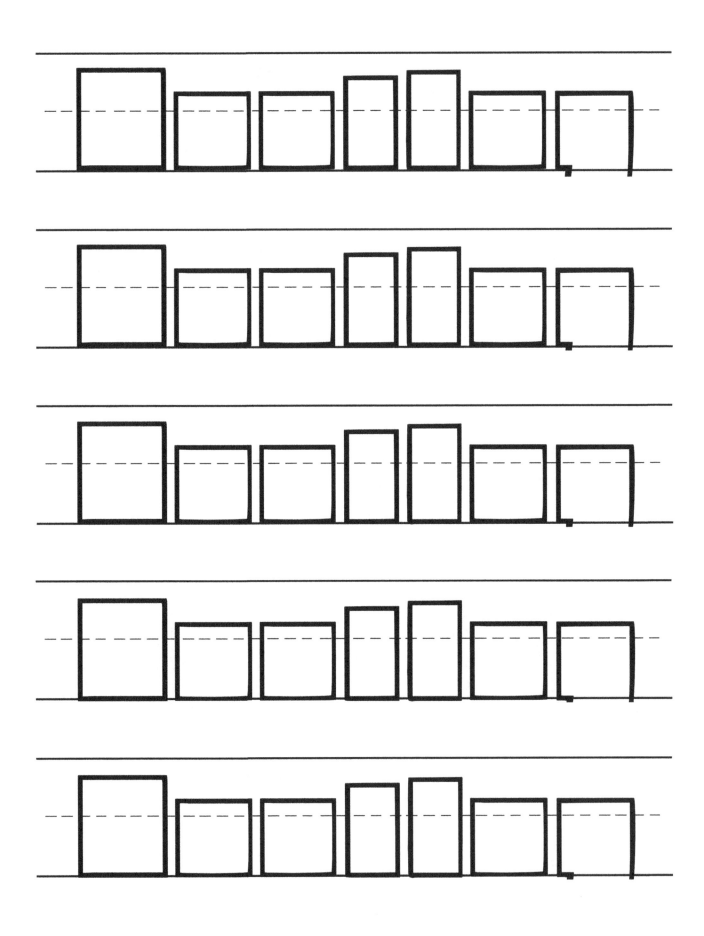

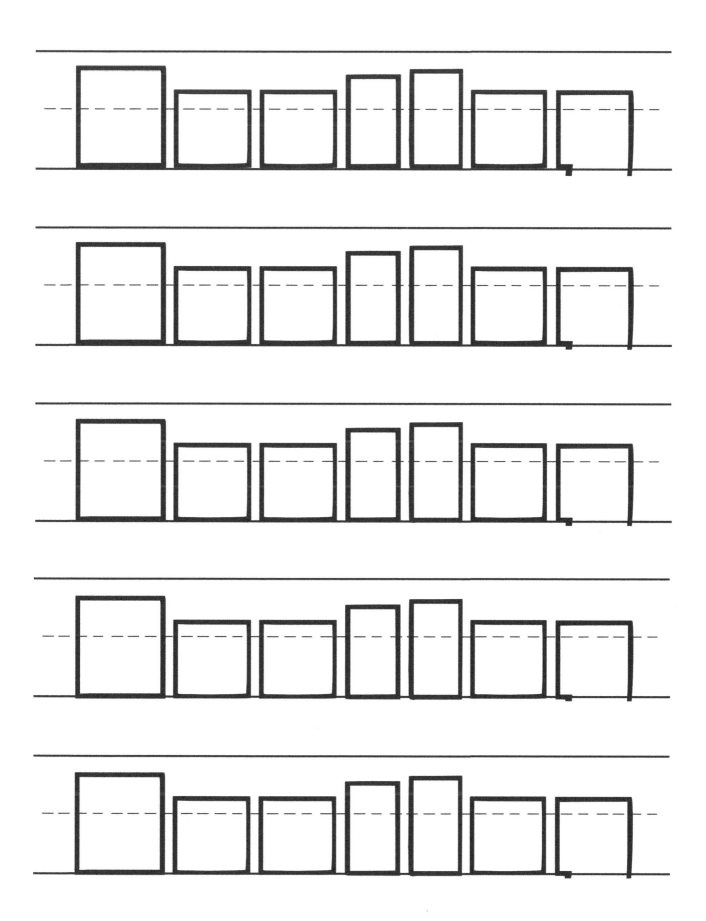

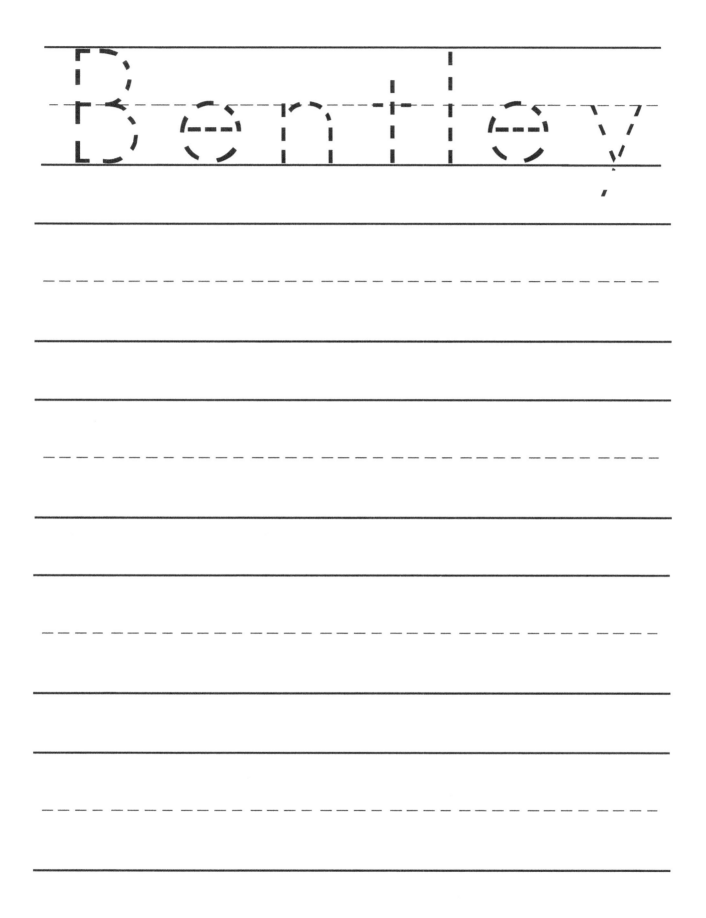

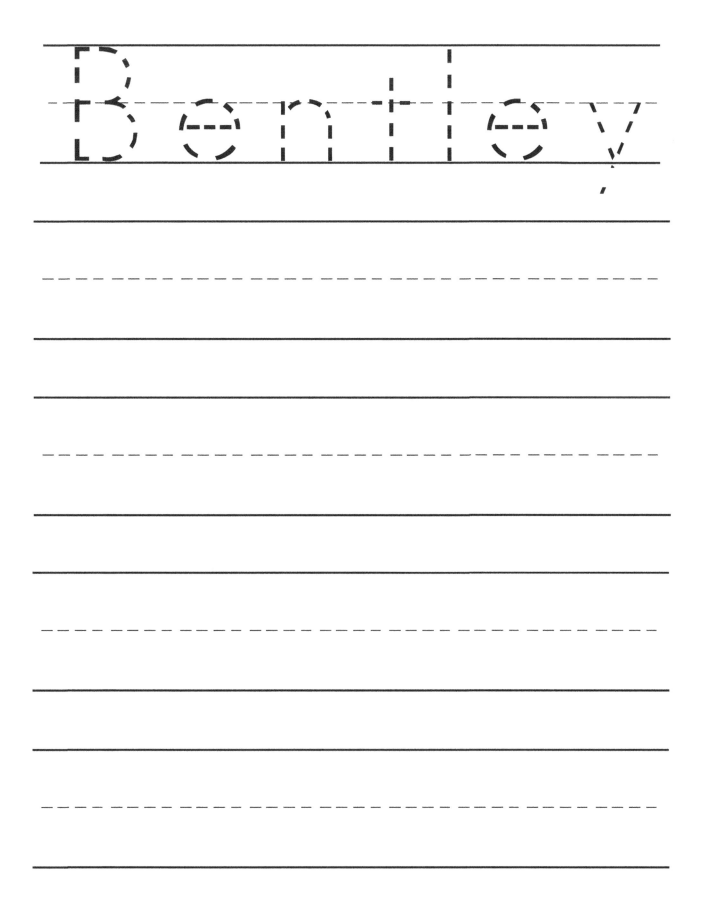

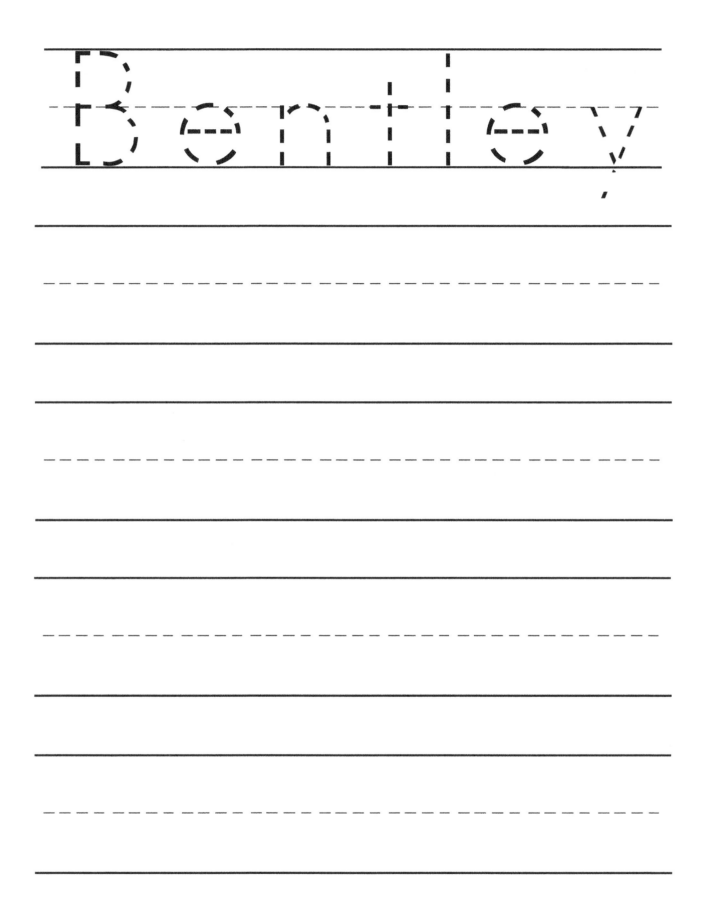

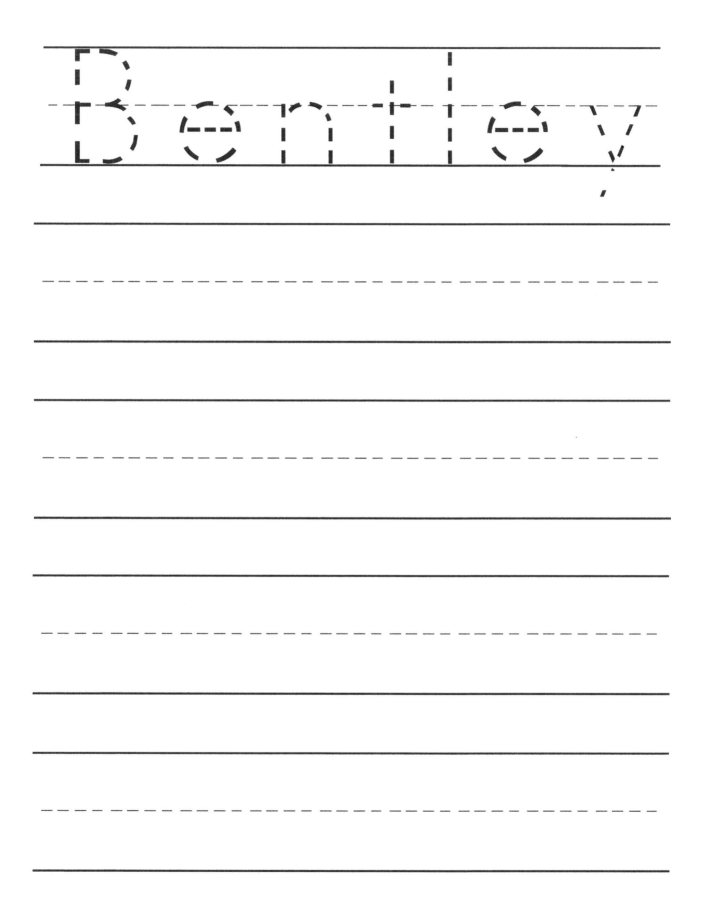

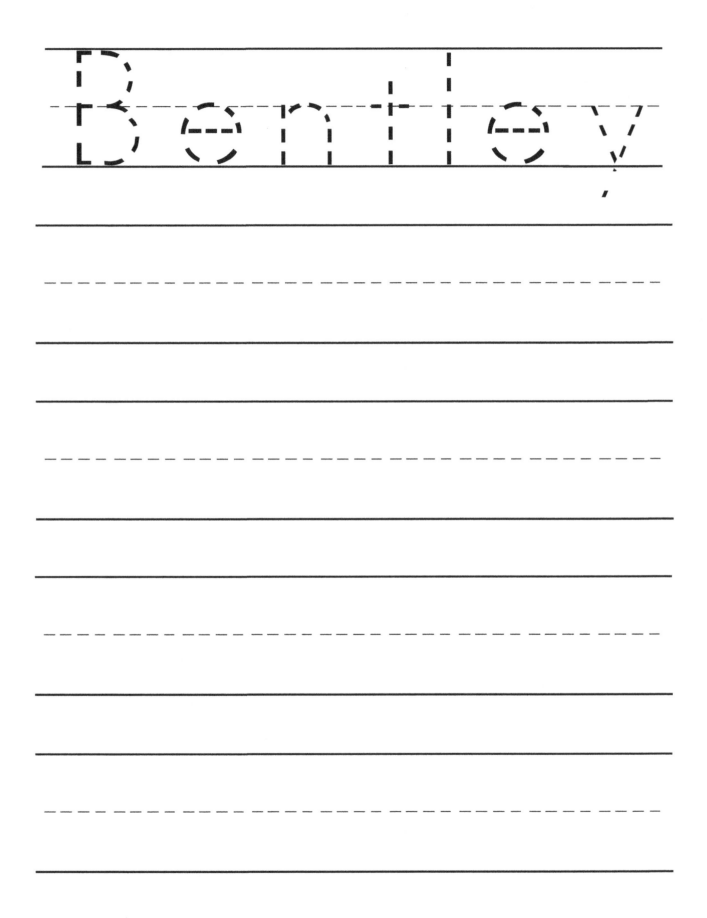

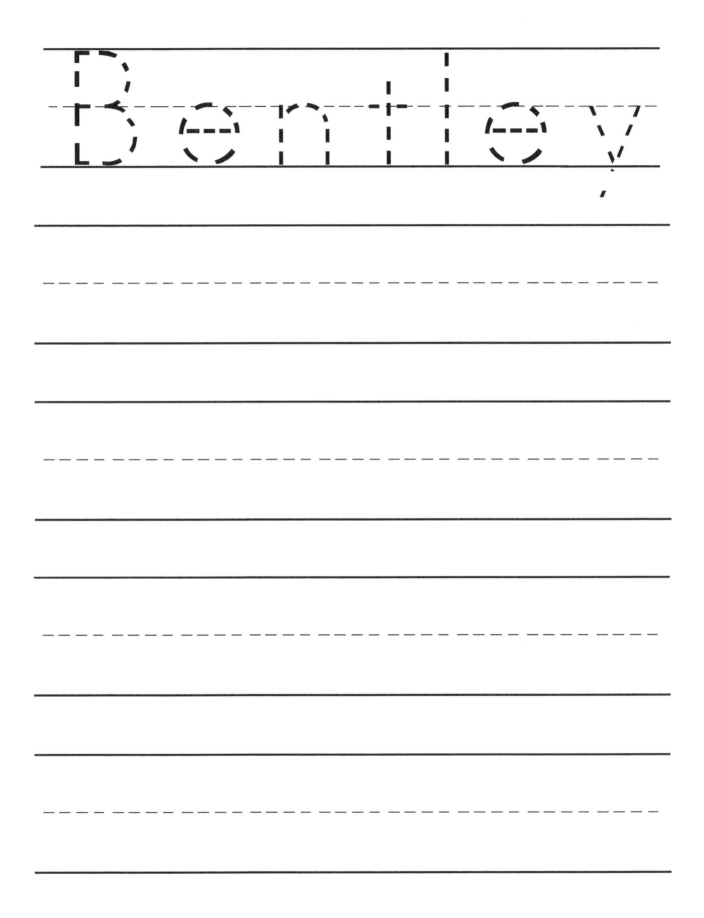

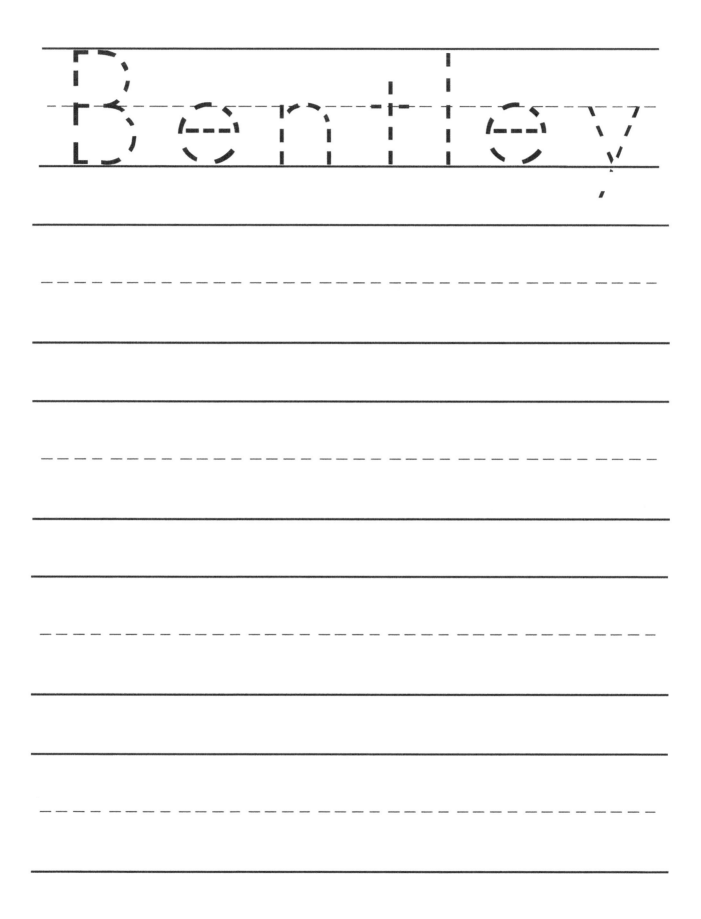

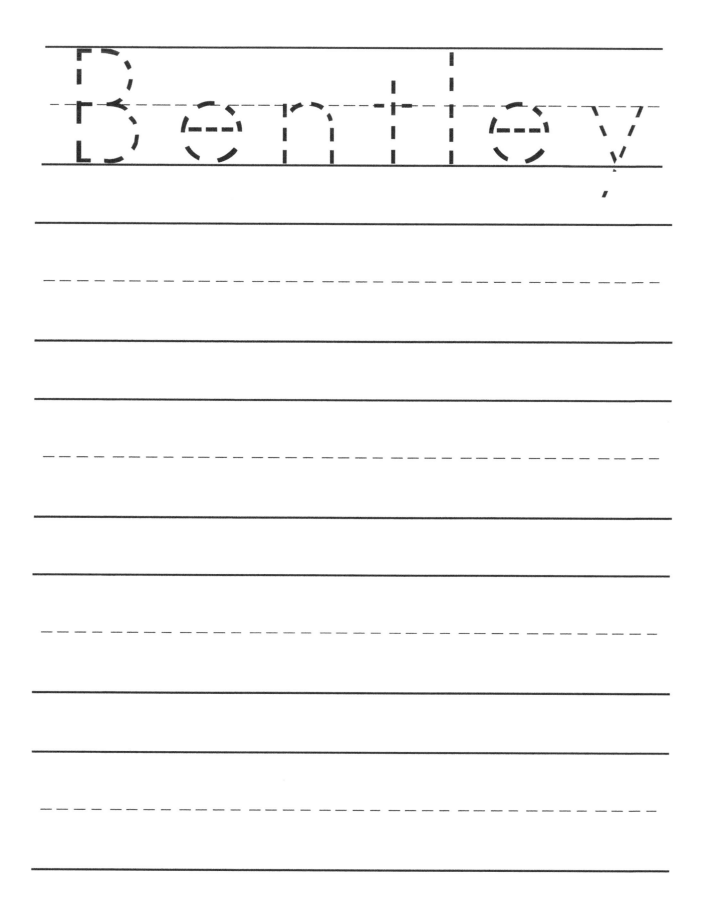

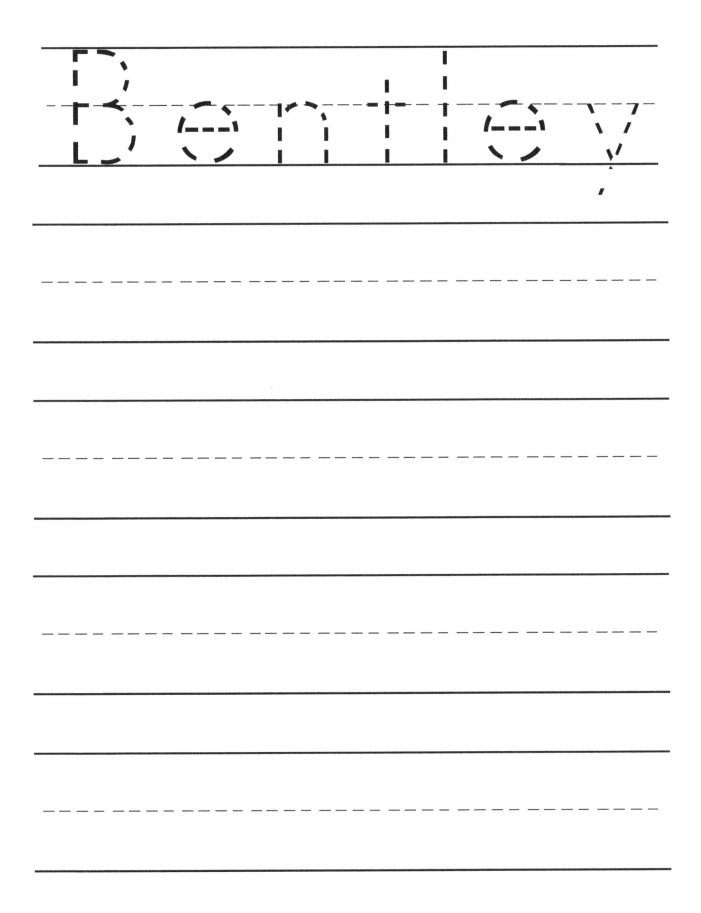

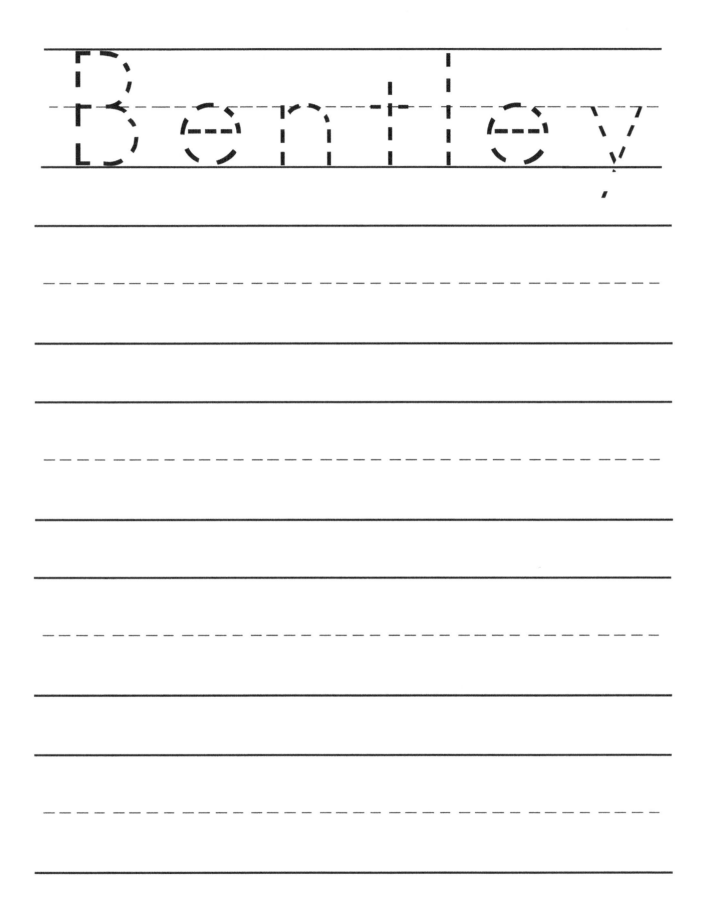

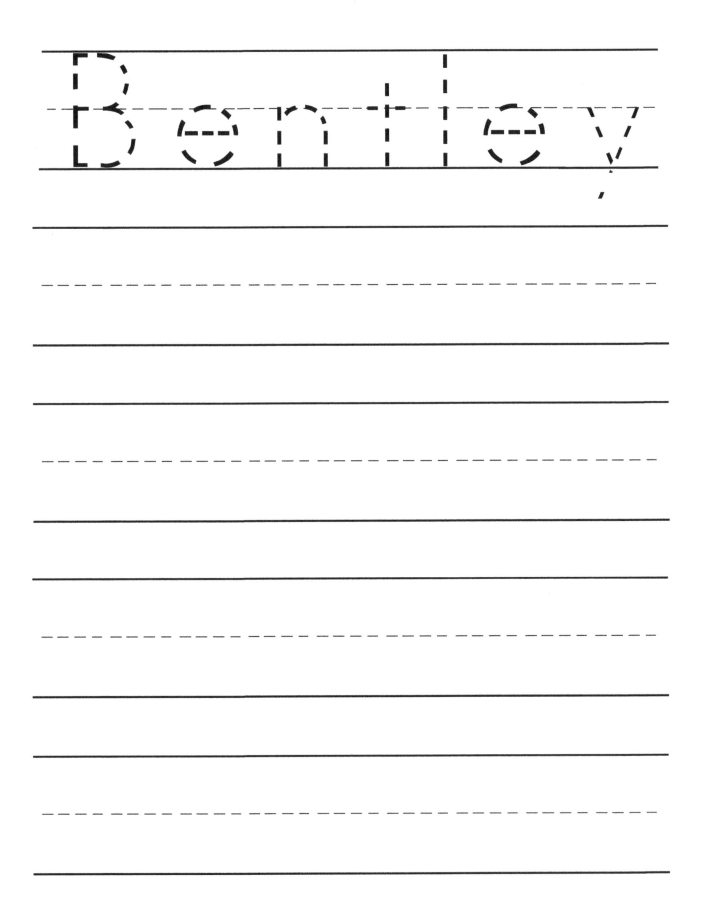

Made in the USA
Columbia, SC
13 December 2019